HAL•LEONARD

JAZZ PLAY-ALONG®

Book and CD for B♭, E♭, C and Bass Clef Instruments

volume 85

Arranged and Produced by
Mark Taylor and Jim Roberts

MOTOWN *Hits*
10 FAVORITE TUNES

BOOK

TITLE	PAGE NUMBERS			
	C Treble Instruments	B♭ Instruments	E♭ Instruments	C Bass Instruments
Ain't Nothing Like the Real Thing	4	18	30	44
Baby I Need Your Lovin'	6	17	32	43
Ben	8	20	34	46
Heatwave (Love Is Like a Heatwave)	7	22	33	48
Mercy, Mercy Me (The Ecology)	10	23	36	49
My Guy	12	24	38	50
Ooo Baby Baby	11	26	37	52
Reach Out, I'll Be There	14	27	40	53
Signed, Sealed, Delivered I'm Yours	15	28	41	54
What's Going On	16	29	42	55

CD

TITLE	CD Track Number Split Track / Melody	CD Track Number Full Stereo Track
Ain't Nothing Like the Real Thing	1	2
Baby I Need Your Lovin'	3	4
Ben	5	6
Heatwave (Love Is Like a Heatwave)	7	8
Mercy, Mercy Me (The Ecology)	9	10
My Guy	11	12
Ooo Baby Baby	13	14
Reach Out, I'll Be There	15	16
Signed, Sealed, Delivered I'm Yours	17	18
What's Going On	19	20
B♭ Tuning Notes		21

ISBN 978-1-4234-5470-0

HAL•LEONARD®
CORPORATION

7777 W. BLUEMOUND RD. P.O. BOX 13819 MILWAUKEE, WI 53213

T0066087

For all works contained herein:
Unauthorized copying, arranging, adapting, recording or public performance is an infringement of copyright.
Infringers are liable under the law.

Visit Hal Leonard Online at
www.halleonard.com

MOTOWN HITS

Volume 85

Arranged and Produced by
Mark Taylor and Jim Roberts

Featured Players:

Graham Breedlove–Trumpet
John Desalme–Saxophone
Tony Nalker–Piano
Jim Roberts–Guitar
Regan Brough–Bass
Steve Fidyk–Drums

Recorded at Bias Studios, Springfield, Virginia
Bob Dawson, Engineer

HOW TO USE THE CD:

Each song has <u>two</u> tracks:

1) Split Track/Melody

Woodwind, Brass, Keyboard, and **Mallet Players** can use this track as a learning tool for melody style and inflection.

Bass Players can learn and perform with this track – remove the recorded bass track by turning down the volume on the LEFT channel.

Keyboard and **Guitar Players** can learn and perform with this track – remove the recorded piano part by turning down the volume on the RIGHT channel.

2) Full Stereo Track

Soloists or **Groups** can learn and perform with this accompaniment track with the RHYTHM SECTION only.

AIN'T NOTHING LIKE THE REAL THING

CD
1 : SPLIT TRACK/MELODY
2 : FULL STEREO TRACK

WORDS AND MUSIC BY NICKOLAS ASHFORD
AND VALERIE SIMPSON

C VERSION

© 1967, 1968, 1974 (Renewed 1995, 1996, 2002) JOBETE MUSIC CO., INC.
This arrangement © 2008 JOBETE MUSIC CO., INC.
All Rights Controlled and Administered by EMI APRIL MUSIC INC.
All Rights Reserved   International Copyright Secured   Used by Permission

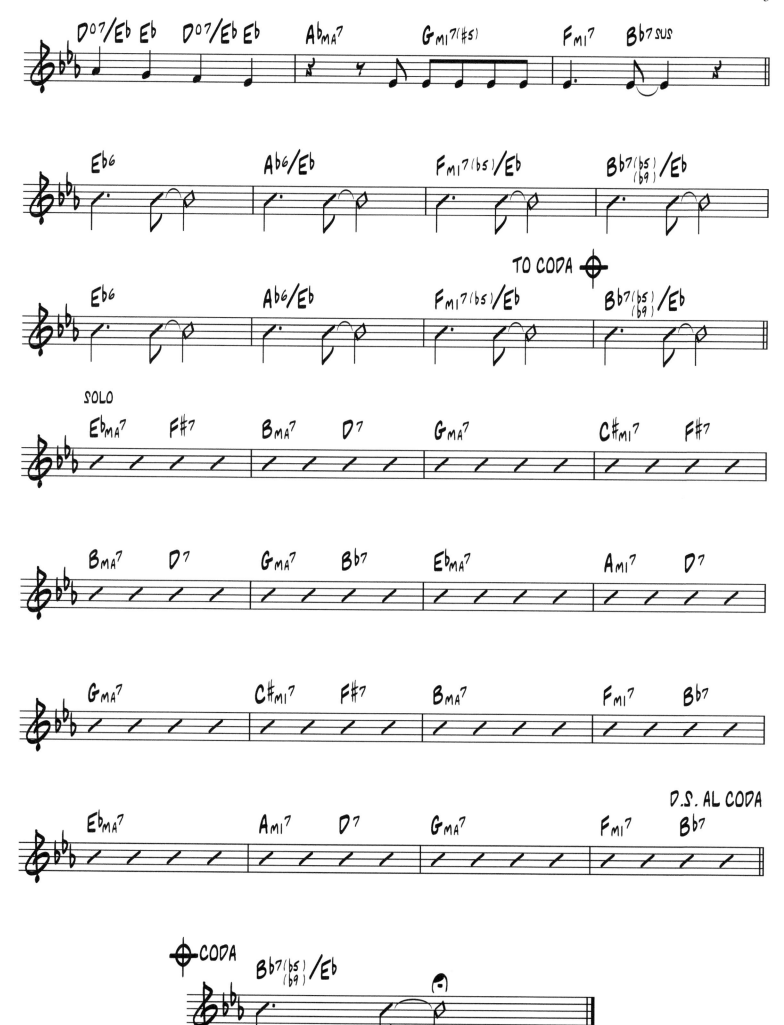

BABY I NEED YOUR LOVIN'

© 1964 (Renewed 1992) JOBETE MUSIC CO., INC.
This arrangement © 2008 JOBETE MUSIC CO., INC.
All Rights Controlled and Administered by EMI BLACKWOOD MUSIC INC. on behalf of STONE AGATE MUSIC (A Division of JOBETE MUSIC CO., INC.)
All Rights Reserved   International Copyright Secured   Used by Permission

CD
◆7: SPLIT TRACK/MELODY
◆8: FULL STEREO TRACK

HEATWAVE
(LOVE IS LIKE A HEATWAVE)

C VERSION

WORDS AND MUSIC BY EDWARD HOLLAND,
LAMONT DOZIER AND BRIAN HOLLAND

© 1963 (Renewed 1991) JOBETE MUSIC CO., INC.
This arrangement © 2008 JOBETE MUSIC CO., INC.
All Rights Controlled and Administered by EMI BLACKWOOD MUSIC INC. on behalf of STONE AGATE MUSIC (A Division of JOBETE MUSIC CO., INC.)
All Rights Reserved   International Copyright Secured   Used by Permission

BEN

WORDS BY DON BLACK
MUSIC BY WALTER SCHARF

CD
- ◆5 : SPLIT TRACK/MELODY
- ◆6 : FULL STEREO TRACK

C VERSION

© 1971, 1972 (Renewed 1999, 2000) JOBETE MUSIC CO., INC.
This arrangement © 2008 JOBETE MUSIC CO., INC.
All Rights Controlled and Administered by EMI APRIL MUSIC INC.
All Rights Reserved International Copyright Secured Used by Permission

MERCY, MERCY ME
(THE ECOLOGY)

WORDS AND MUSIC BY
MARVIN GAYE

© 1971 (Renewed 1999) JOBETE MUSIC CO., INC.
This arrangement © 2008 JOBETE MUSIC CO., INC.
All Rights Controlled and Administered by EMI APRIL MUSIC INC.
All Rights Reserved   International Copyright Secured   Used by Permission

OOO Baby Baby

WORDS AND MUSIC BY WILLIAM "SMOKEY" ROBINSON
AND WARREN MOORE

CD
- **13** : SPLIT TRACK/MELODY
- **14** : FULL STEREO TRACK

C VERSION

© 1965, 1972 (Renewed 1993, 2000) JOBETE MUSIC CO., INC.
This arrangement © 2008 JOBETE MUSIC CO., INC.
All Rights Controlled and Administered by EMI APRIL MUSIC INC.
All Rights Reserved   International Copyright Secured   Used by Permission

MY GUY

WORDS AND MUSIC BY
WILLIAM "SMOKEY" ROBINSON

© 1964 (Renewed 1992) JOBETE MUSIC CO., INC.
This arrangement © 2008 JOBETE MUSIC CO., INC.
All Rights Controlled and Administered by EMI APRIL MUSIC INC.
All Rights Reserved International Copyright Secured Used by Permission

REACH OUT, I'LL BE THERE

WORDS AND MUSIC BY BRIAN HOLLAND,
LAMONT DOZIER AND EDWARD HOLLAND

C VERSION

© 1966 (Renewed 1994) JOBETE MUSIC CO., INC.
This arrangement © 2008 JOBETE MUSIC CO., INC.
All Rights Controlled and Administered by EMI BLACKWOOD MUSIC INC. on behalf of STONE AGATE MUSIC (A Division of JOBETE MUSIC CO., INC.)
All Rights Reserved   International Copyright Secured   Used by Permission

Signed, Sealed, Delivered I'm Yours

WORDS AND MUSIC BY STEVIE WONDER, SYREETA WRIGHT, LEE GARRETT AND LULA MAE HARDAWAY

© 1970 (Renewed 1998) JOBETE MUSIC CO., INC., BLACK BULL MUSIC and SAWANDI MUSIC c/o EMI APRIL MUSIC INC. and EMI BLACKWOOD MUSIC INC.
This arrangement © 2008 JOBETE MUSIC CO., INC., BLACK BULL MUSIC and SAWANDI MUSIC c/o EMI APRIL MUSIC INC. and EMI BLACKWOOD MUSIC INC.
All Rights Reserved   International Copyright Secured   Used by Permission

WHAT'S GOING ON

CD
19 : SPLIT TRACK/MELODY
20 : FULL STEREO TRACK

WORDS AND MUSIC BY MARVIN GAYE,
AL CLEVELAND AND RENALDO BENSON

C VERSION

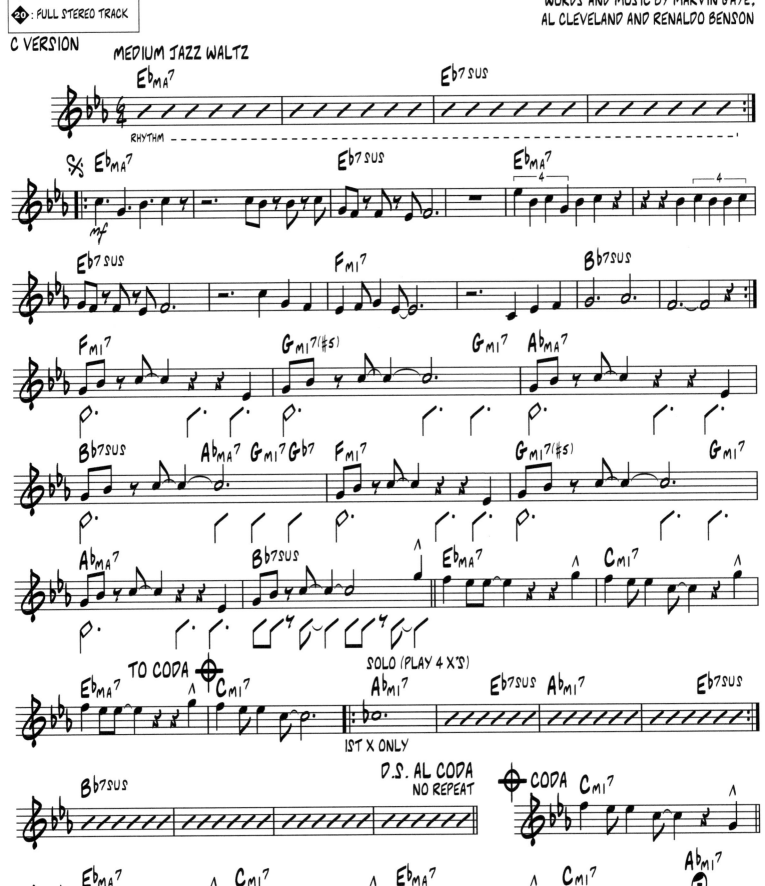

© 1970, 1971, 1972 (Renewed 1998, 1999, 2000) JOBETE MUSIC CO., INC.
This arrangement © 2008 JOBETE MUSIC CO., INC.
All Rights Controlled and Administered by EMI APRIL MUSIC INC. and EMI BLACKWOOD MUSIC INC. on behalf of JOBETE MUSIC CO., INC.
and STONE AGATE MUSIC (A Division of JOBETE MUSIC CO., INC.)
All Rights Reserved   International Copyright Secured   Used by Permission

BABY I NEED YOUR LOVIN'

WORDS AND MUSIC BY BRIAN HOLLAND, LAMONT DOZIER AND EDWARD HOLLAND

© 1964 (Renewed 1992) JOBETE MUSIC CO., INC.
This arrangement © 2008 JOBETE MUSIC CO., INC.
All Rights Controlled and Administered by EMI BLACKWOOD MUSIC INC. on behalf of STONE AGATE MUSIC (A Division of JOBETE MUSIC CO., INC.)
All Rights Reserved   International Copyright Secured   Used by Permission

AIN'T NOTHING LIKE THE REAL THING

WORDS AND MUSIC BY NICKOLAS ASHFORD
AND VALERIE SIMPSON

CD
❶ : SPLIT TRACK/MELODY
❷ : FULL STEREO TRACK

Bb VERSION

© 1967, 1968, 1974 (Renewed 1995, 1996, 2002) JOBETE MUSIC CO., INC.
This arrangement © 2008 JOBETE MUSIC CO., INC.
All Rights Controlled and Administered by EMI APRIL MUSIC INC.
All Rights Reserved International Copyright Secured Used by Permission

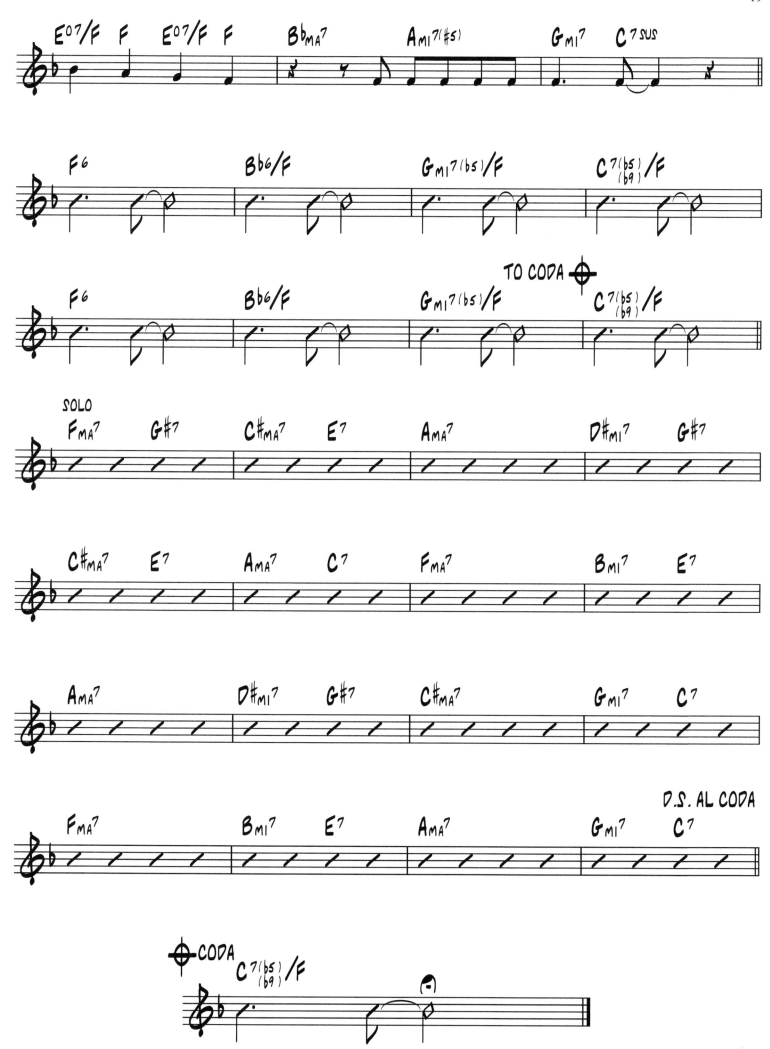

BEN

WORDS BY DON BLACK
MUSIC BY WALTER SCHARF

Bb VERSION

© 1971, 1972 (Renewed 1999, 2000) JOBETE MUSIC CO., INC.
This arrangement © 2008 JOBETE MUSIC CO., INC.
All Rights Controlled and Administered by EMI APRIL MUSIC INC.
All Rights Reserved   International Copyright Secured   Used by Permission

HEATWAVE
(LOVE IS LIKE A HEATWAVE)

WORDS AND MUSIC BY EDWARD HOLLAND,
LAMONT DOZIER AND BRIAN HOLLAND

Bb VERSION

© 1963 (Renewed 1991) JOBETE MUSIC CO., INC.
This arrangement © 2008 JOBETE MUSIC CO., INC.
All Rights Controlled and Administered by EMI BLACKWOOD MUSIC INC. on behalf of STONE AGATE MUSIC (A Division of JOBETE MUSIC CO., INC.)
All Rights Reserved   International Copyright Secured   Used by Permission

Mercy, Mercy Me
(The Ecology)

Words and Music by
Marvin Gaye

CD
9 : Split Track/Melody
10 : Full Stereo Track

23

© 1971 (Renewed 1999) Jobete Music Co., Inc.
This arrangement © 2008 Jobete Music Co., Inc.
All Rights Controlled and Administered by EMI April Music Inc.
All Rights Reserved International Copyright Secured Used by Permission

MY GUY

WORDS AND MUSIC BY
WILLIAM "SMOKEY" ROBINSON

© 1964 (Renewed 1992) JOBETE MUSIC CO., INC.
This arrangement © 2008 JOBETE MUSIC CO., INC.
All Rights Controlled and Administered by EMI APRIL MUSIC INC.
All Rights Reserved   International Copyright Secured   Used by Permission

Ooo Baby Baby

WORDS AND MUSIC BY WILLIAM "SMOKEY" ROBINSON
AND WARREN MOORE

© 1965, 1972 (Renewed 1993, 2000) JOBETE MUSIC CO., INC.
This arrangement © 2008 JOBETE MUSIC CO., INC.
All Rights Controlled and Administered by EMI APRIL MUSIC INC.
All Rights Reserved International Copyright Secured Used by Permission

REACH OUT, I'LL BE THERE

WORDS AND MUSIC BY BRIAN HOLLAND,
LAMONT DOZIER AND EDWARD HOLLAND

CD
15: SPLIT TRACK/MELODY
16: FULL STEREO TRACK

Bb VERSION

© 1966 (Renewed 1994) JOBETE MUSIC CO., INC.
This arrangement © 2008 JOBETE MUSIC CO., INC.
All Rights Controlled and Administered by EMI BLACKWOOD MUSIC INC. on behalf of STONE AGATE MUSIC (A Division of JOBETE MUSIC CO., INC.)
All Rights Reserved   International Copyright Secured   Used by Permission

CD
17: SPLIT TRACK/MELODY
18: FULL STEREO TRACK

SIGNED, SEALED, DELIVERED I'M YOURS

WORDS AND MUSIC BY STEVIE WONDER, SYREETA WRIGHT,
LEE GARRETT AND LULA MAE HARDAWAY

© 1970 (Renewed 1998) JOBETE MUSIC CO., INC., BLACK BULL MUSIC and SAWANDI MUSIC c/o EMI APRIL MUSIC INC. and EMI BLACKWOOD MUSIC INC.
This arrangement © 2008 JOBETE MUSIC CO., INC., BLACK BULL MUSIC and SAWANDI MUSIC c/o EMI APRIL MUSIC INC. and EMI BLACKWOOD MUSIC INC.
All Rights Reserved   International Copyright Secured   Used by Permission

WHAT'S GOING ON

WORDS AND MUSIC BY MARVIN GAYE,
AL CLEVELAND AND RENALDO BENSON

© 1970, 1971, 1972 (Renewed 1998, 1999, 2000) JOBETE MUSIC CO., INC.
This arrangement © 2008 JOBETE MUSIC CO., INC.
All Rights Controlled and Administered by EMI APRIL MUSIC INC. and EMI BLACKWOOD MUSIC INC. on behalf of JOBETE MUSIC CO., INC.
and STONE AGATE MUSIC (A Division of JOBETE MUSIC CO., INC.)
All Rights Reserved   International Copyright Secured   Used by Permission

AIN'T NOTHING LIKE THE REAL THING

© 1967, 1968, 1974 (Renewed 1995, 1996, 2002) JOBETE MUSIC CO., INC.
This arrangement © 2008 JOBETE MUSIC CO., INC.
All Rights Controlled and Administered by EMI APRIL MUSIC INC.
All Rights Reserved International Copyright Secured Used by Permission

BABY I NEED YOUR LOVIN'

WORDS AND MUSIC BY BRIAN HOLLAND,
LAMONT DOZIER AND EDWARD HOLLAND

© 1964 (Renewed 1992) JOBETE MUSIC CO., INC.
This arrangement © 2008 JOBETE MUSIC CO., INC.
All Rights Controlled and Administered by EMI BLACKWOOD MUSIC INC. on behalf of STONE AGATE MUSIC (A Division of JOBETE MUSIC CO., INC.)
All Rights Reserved   International Copyright Secured   Used by Permission

HEATWAVE
(LOVE IS LIKE A HEATWAVE)

CD

◆ 7 : SPLIT TRACK/MELODY
◆ 8 : FULL STEREO TRACK

Eb VERSION

WORDS AND MUSIC BY EDWARD HOLLAND,
LAMONT DOZIER AND BRIAN HOLLAND

© 1963 (Renewed 1991) JOBETE MUSIC CO., INC.
This arrangement © 2008 JOBETE MUSIC CO., INC.
All Rights Controlled and Administered by EMI BLACKWOOD MUSIC INC. on behalf of STONE AGATE MUSIC (A Division of JOBETE MUSIC CO., INC.)
All Rights Reserved   International Copyright Secured   Used by Permission

BEN

WORDS BY DON BLACK
MUSIC BY WALTER SCHARF

© 1971, 1972 (Renewed 1999, 2000) JOBETE MUSIC CO., INC.
This arrangement © 2008 JOBETE MUSIC CO., INC.
All Rights Controlled and Administered by EMI APRIL MUSIC INC.
All Rights Reserved   International Copyright Secured   Used by Permission

MERCY, MERCY ME
(THE ECOLOGY)

WORDS AND MUSIC BY
MARVIN GAYE

Eb VERSION

MEDIUM ROCK BALLAD

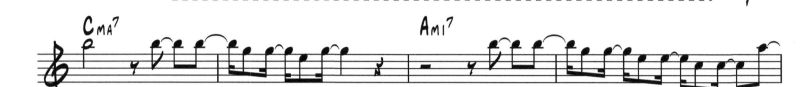

SOLOS (6 CHORUSES)

1ST X ONLY

© 1971 (Renewed 1999) JOBETE MUSIC CO., INC.
This arrangement © 2008 JOBETE MUSIC CO., INC.
All Rights Controlled and Administered by EMI APRIL MUSIC INC.
All Rights Reserved   International Copyright Secured   Used by Permission

OOO BABY BABY

WORDS AND MUSIC BY WILLIAM "SMOKEY" ROBINSON
AND WARREN MOORE

© 1965, 1972 (Renewed 1993, 2000) JOBETE MUSIC CO., INC.
This arrangement © 2008 JOBETE MUSIC CO., INC.
All Rights Controlled and Administered by EMI APRIL MUSIC INC.
All Rights Reserved International Copyright Secured Used by Permission

MY GUY

WORDS AND MUSIC BY
WILLIAM "SMOKEY" ROBINSON

© 1964 (Renewed 1992) JOBETE MUSIC CO., INC.
This arrangement © 2008 JOBETE MUSIC CO., INC.
All Rights Controlled and Administered by EMI APRIL MUSIC INC.
All Rights Reserved   International Copyright Secured   Used by Permission

CD

REACH OUT, I'LL BE THERE

WORDS AND MUSIC BY BRIAN HOLLAND,
LAMONT DOZIER AND EDWARD HOLLAND

Eb VERSION

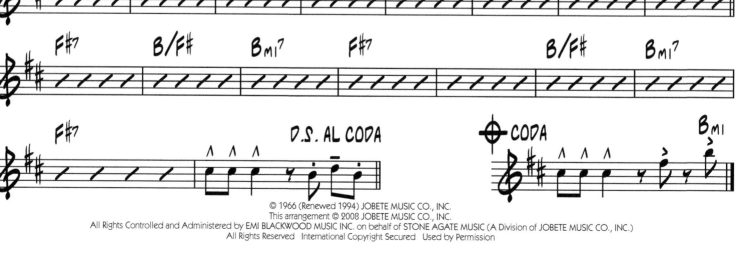

© 1966 (Renewed 1994) JOBETE MUSIC CO., INC.
This arrangement © 2008 JOBETE MUSIC CO., INC.
All Rights Controlled and Administered by EMI BLACKWOOD MUSIC INC. on behalf of STONE AGATE MUSIC (A Division of JOBETE MUSIC CO., INC.)
All Rights Reserved International Copyright Secured Used by Permission

Signed, Sealed, Delivered I'm Yours

WORDS AND MUSIC BY STEVIE WONDER, SYREETA WRIGHT,
LEE GARRETT AND LULA MAE HARDAWAY

© 1970 (Renewed 1998) JOBETE MUSIC CO., INC., BLACK BULL MUSIC and SAWANDI MUSIC c/o EMI APRIL MUSIC INC. and EMI BLACKWOOD MUSIC INC.
This arrangement © 2008 JOBETE MUSIC CO., INC., BLACK BULL MUSIC and SAWANDI MUSIC c/o EMI APRIL MUSIC INC. and EMI BLACKWOOD MUSIC INC.
All Rights Reserved   International Copyright Secured   Used by Permission

WHAT'S GOING ON

WORDS AND MUSIC BY MARVIN GAYE,
AL CLEVELAND AND RENALDO BENSON

CD
19 : SPLIT TRACK/MELODY
20 : FULL STEREO TRACK

Eb VERSION   MEDIUM JAZZ WALTZ

© 1970, 1971, 1972 (Renewed 1998, 1999, 2000) JOBETE MUSIC CO., INC.
This arrangement © 2008 JOBETE MUSIC CO., INC.
All Rights Controlled and Administered by EMI APRIL MUSIC INC. and EMI BLACKWOOD MUSIC INC. on behalf of JOBETE MUSIC CO., INC.
and STONE AGATE MUSIC (A Division of JOBETE MUSIC CO., INC.)
All Rights Reserved   International Copyright Secured   Used by Permission

BABY I NEED YOUR LOVIN'

WORDS AND MUSIC BY BRIAN HOLLAND,
LAMONT DOZIER AND EDWARD HOLLAND

CD
◆ : SPLIT TRACK/MELODY
◄ : FULL STEREO TRACK

𝄢: C VERSION

© 1964 (Renewed 1992) JOBETE MUSIC CO., INC.
This arrangement © 2008 JOBETE MUSIC CO., INC.
All Rights Controlled and Administered by EMI BLACKWOOD MUSIC INC. on behalf of STONE AGATE MUSIC (A Division of JOBETE MUSIC CO., INC.)
All Rights Reserved   International Copyright Secured   Used by Permission

AIN'T NOTHING LIKE THE REAL THING

WORDS AND MUSIC BY NICKOLAS ASHFORD
AND VALERIE SIMPSON

© 1967, 1968, 1974 (Renewed 1995, 1996, 2002) JOBETE MUSIC CO., INC.
This arrangement © 2008 JOBETE MUSIC CO., INC.
All Rights Controlled and Administered by EMI APRIL MUSIC INC.
All Rights Reserved   International Copyright Secured   Used by Permission

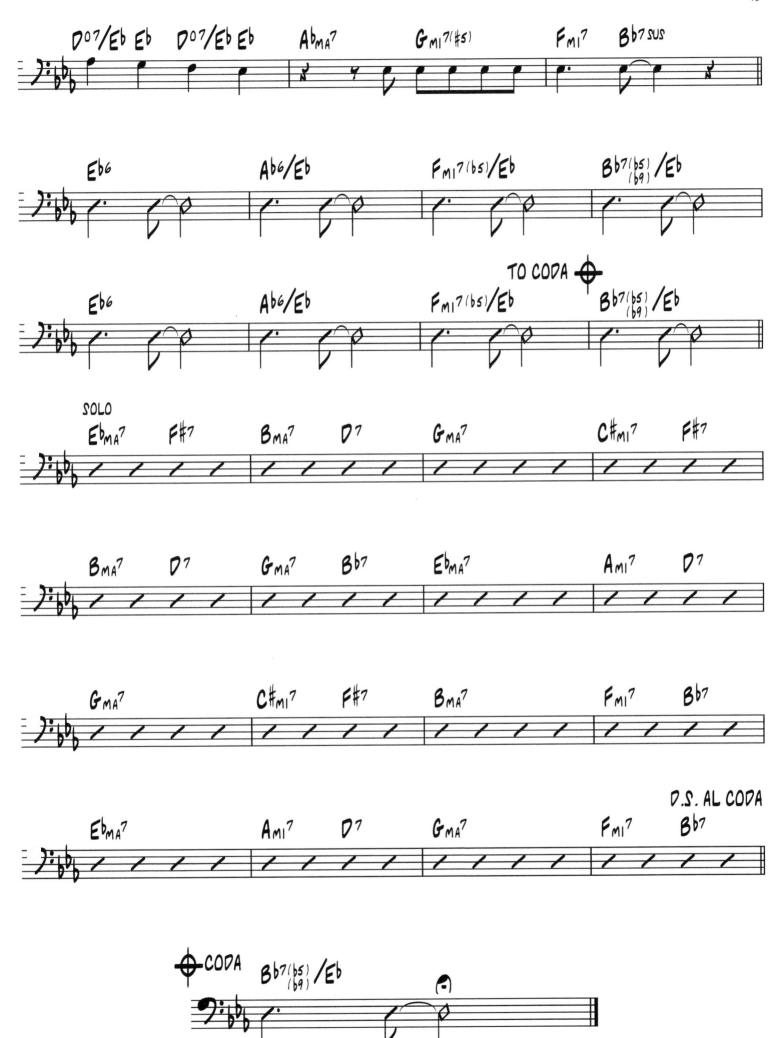

BEN

WORDS BY DON BLACK
MUSIC BY WALTER SCHARF

♪: C VERSION

© 1971, 1972 (Renewed 1999, 2000) JOBETE MUSIC CO., INC.
This arrangement © 2008 JOBETE MUSIC CO., INC.
All Rights Controlled and Administered by EMI APRIL MUSIC INC.
All Rights Reserved   International Copyright Secured   Used by Permission

CD

◀ : SPLIT TRACK/MELODY
◀ : FULL STEREO TRACK

𝄢: C VERSION

HEATWAVE
(LOVE IS LIKE A HEATWAVE)

WORDS AND MUSIC BY EDWARD HOLLAND,
LAMONT DOZIER AND BRIAN HOLLAND

© 1963 (Renewed 1991) JOBETE MUSIC CO., INC.
This arrangement © 2008 JOBETE MUSIC CO., INC.
All Rights Controlled and Administered by EMI BLACKWOOD MUSIC INC. on behalf of STONE AGATE MUSIC (A Division of JOBETE MUSIC CO., INC.)
All Rights Reserved   International Copyright Secured   Used by Permission

MERCY, MERCY ME
(THE ECOLOGY)

WORDS AND MUSIC BY
MARVIN GAYE

© 1971 (Renewed 1999) JOBETE MUSIC CO., INC.
This arrangement © 2008 JOBETE MUSIC CO., INC.
All Rights Controlled and Administered by EMI APRIL MUSIC INC.
All Rights Reserved   International Copyright Secured   Used by Permission

MY GUY

WORDS AND MUSIC BY
WILLIAM "SMOKEY" ROBINSON

CD
🎵11: SPLIT TRACK/MELODY
🎵12: FULL STEREO TRACK

𝄢: C VERSION

© 1964 (Renewed 1992) JOBETE MUSIC CO., INC.
This arrangement © 2008 JOBETE MUSIC CO., INC.
All Rights Controlled and Administered by EMI APRIL MUSIC INC.
All Rights Reserved International Copyright Secured Used by Permission

OOO BABY BABY

WORDS AND MUSIC BY WILLIAM "SMOKEY" ROBINSON
AND WARREN MOORE

© 1965, 1972 (Renewed 1993, 2000) JOBETE MUSIC CO., INC.
This arrangement © 2008 JOBETE MUSIC CO., INC.
All Rights Controlled and Administered by EMI APRIL MUSIC INC.
All Rights Reserved International Copyright Secured Used by Permission

Reach Out, I'll Be There

WORDS AND MUSIC BY BRIAN HOLLAND,
LAMONT DOZIER AND EDWARD HOLLAND

© 1966 (Renewed 1994) JOBETE MUSIC CO., INC.
This arrangement © 2008 JOBETE MUSIC CO., INC.
All Rights Controlled and Administered by EMI BLACKWOOD MUSIC INC. on behalf of STONE AGATE MUSIC (A Division of JOBETE MUSIC CO., INC.)
All Rights Reserved   International Copyright Secured   Used by Permission

SIGNED, SEALED, DELIVERED I'M YOURS

WORDS AND MUSIC BY STEVIE WONDER, SYREETA WRIGHT,
LEE GARRETT AND LULA MAE HARDAWAY

© 1970 (Renewed 1998) JOBETE MUSIC CO., INC., BLACK BULL MUSIC and SAWANDI MUSIC c/o EMI APRIL MUSIC INC. and EMI BLACKWOOD MUSIC INC.
This arrangement © 2008 JOBETE MUSIC CO., INC., BLACK BULL MUSIC and SAWANDI MUSIC c/o EMI APRIL MUSIC INC. and EMI BLACKWOOD MUSIC INC.
All Rights Reserved   International Copyright Secured   Used by Permission

WHAT'S GOING ON

WORDS AND MUSIC BY MARVIN GAYE,
AL CLEVELAND AND RENALDO BENSON

© 1970, 1971, 1972 (Renewed 1998, 1999, 2000) JOBETE MUSIC CO., INC.
This arrangement © 2008 JOBETE MUSIC CO., INC.
All Rights Controlled and Administered by EMI APRIL MUSIC INC. and EMI BLACKWOOD MUSIC INC. on behalf of JOBETE MUSIC CO., INC.
and STONE AGATE MUSIC (A Division of JOBETE MUSIC CO., INC.)
All Rights Reserved International Copyright Secured Used by Permission

Presenting the Hal Leonard JAZZ PLAY-ALONG® SERIES

1. DUKE ELLINGTON
00841644 .... $16.95

1A. MAIDEN VOYAGE/ALL BLUES
00843158 .... $15.99

2. MILES DAVIS
00841645 .... $16.95

3. THE BLUES
00841646 .... $16.99

4. JAZZ BALLADS
00841691 .... $16.99

5. BEST OF BEBOP
00841689 .... $16.99

6. JAZZ CLASSICS WITH EASY CHANGES
00841690 .... $16.99

7. ESSENTIAL JAZZ STANDARDS
00843000 .... $16.99

8. ANTONIO CARLOS JOBIM AND THE ART OF THE BOSSA NOVA
00843001 .... $16.95

9. DIZZY GILLESPIE
00843002 .... $16.99

10. DISNEY CLASSICS
00843003 .... $16.99

11. RODGERS AND HART – FAVORITES
00843004 .... $16.99

12. ESSENTIAL JAZZ CLASSICS
00843005 .... $16.99

13. JOHN COLTRANE
00843006 .... $16.95

14. IRVING BERLIN
00843007 .... $15.99

15. RODGERS & HAMMERSTEIN
00843008 .... $15.99

16. COLE PORTER
00843009 .... $15.95

17. COUNT BASIE
00843010 .... $16.95

18. HAROLD ARLEN
00843011 .... $15.95

19. COOL JAZZ
00843012 .... $15.95

20. CHRISTMAS CAROLS
00843080 .... $14.95

21. RODGERS AND HART – CLASSICS
00843014 .... $14.95

22. WAYNE SHORTER
00843015 .... $16.95

23. LATIN JAZZ
00843016 .... $16.95

24. EARLY JAZZ STANDARDS
00843017 .... $14.95

25. CHRISTMAS JAZZ
00843018 .... $16.95

26. CHARLIE PARKER
00843019 .... $16.95

27. GREAT JAZZ STANDARDS
00843020 .... $15.99

28. BIG BAND ERA
00843021 .... $15.99

29. LENNON AND McCARTNEY
00843022 .... $16.95

30. BLUES' BEST
00843023 .... $15.99

31. JAZZ IN THREE
00843024 .... $15.99

32. BEST OF SWING
00843025 .... $15.99

33. SONNY ROLLINS
00843029 .... $15.95

34. ALL TIME STANDARDS
00843030 .... $15.99

35. BLUESY JAZZ
00843031 .... $15.99

36. HORACE SILVER
00843032 .... $16.99

37. BILL EVANS
00843033 .... $16.95

38. YULETIDE JAZZ
00843034 .... $16.95

39. "ALL THE THINGS YOU ARE" & MORE JEROME KERN SONGS
00843035 .... $15.99

40. BOSSA NOVA
00843036 .... $15.99

41. CLASSIC DUKE ELLINGTON
00843037 .... $16.99

42. GERRY MULLIGAN – FAVORITES
00843038 .... $16.99

43. GERRY MULLIGAN – CLASSICS
00843039 .... $16.95

44. OLIVER NELSON
00843040 .... $16.95

45. JAZZ AT THE MOVIES
00843041 .... $15.99

46. BROADWAY JAZZ STANDARDS
00843042 .... $15.99

47. CLASSIC JAZZ BALLADS
00843043 .... $15.99

48. BEBOP CLASSICS
00843044 .... $16.99

49. MILES DAVIS – STANDARDS
00843045 .... $16.95

50. GREAT JAZZ CLASSICS
00843046 .... $15.99

51. UP-TEMPO JAZZ
00843047 .... $15.99

52. STEVIE WONDER
00843048 .... $15.99

53. RHYTHM CHANGES
00843049 .... $15.99

54. "MOONLIGHT IN VERMONT" & OTHER GREAT STANDARDS
00843050 .... $15.99

55. BENNY GOLSON
00843052 .... $15.95

56. "GEORGIA ON MY MIND" & OTHER SONGS BY HOAGY CARMICHAEL
00843056 .... $15.99

57. VINCE GUARALDI
00843057 .... $16.99

58. MORE LENNON AND McCARTNEY
00843059 .... $15.99

59. SOUL JAZZ
00843060 .... $15.99

60. DEXTER GORDON
00843061 .... $15.95

61. MONGO SANTAMARIA
00843062 .... $15.95

62. JAZZ-ROCK FUSION
00843063 .... $14.95

63. CLASSICAL JAZZ
00843064 .... $14.95

64. TV TUNES
00843065 .... $14.95

65. SMOOTH JAZZ
00843066 .... $16.99

66. A CHARLIE BROWN CHRISTMAS
00843067 .... $16.99

67. CHICK COREA
00843068 .... $15.95

68. CHARLES MINGUS
00843069 .... $16.95

69. CLASSIC JAZZ
00843071 .... $15.99

70. THE DOORS
00843072 .... $14.95

71. COLE PORTER CLASSICS
00843073 .... $14.95

72. CLASSIC JAZZ BALLADS
00843074 .... $15.99

73. JAZZ/BLUES
00843075 .... $14.95

74. BEST JAZZ CLASSICS
00843076 .... $15.99

75. PAUL DESMOND
00843077 .... $14.95

76. BROADWAY JAZZ BALLADS
00843078 .... $15.99

77. JAZZ ON BROADWAY
00843079 .... $15.99

78. STEELY DAN
00843070 .... $14.99

79. MILES DAVIS – CLASSICS
00843081 .... $15.99

80. JIMI HENDRIX
00843083 .... $15.99

81. FRANK SINATRA – CLASSICS
00843084 .... $15.99

82. FRANK SINATRA – STANDARDS
00843085 .... $15.99

83. ANDREW LLOYD WEBBER
00843104 .... $14.95

84. BOSSA NOVA CLASSICS
00843105 .... $14.95

85. MOTOWN HITS
00843109 .... $14.95

86. BENNY GOODMAN
00843110 .... $14.95

87. DIXIELAND
00843111 .... $14.95

88. DUKE ELLINGTON FAVORITES
00843112 .... $14.95

89. IRVING BERLIN FAVORITES
00843113 .... $14.95

90. THELONIOUS MONK CLASSICS
00841262 .... $16.99

91. THELONIOUS MONK FAVORITES
00841263 .... $16.99

92. LEONARD BERNSTEIN
00450134 .... $15.99

93. DISNEY FAVORITES
00843142 .... $14.99

94. RAY
00843143 .... $14.99

95. JAZZ AT THE LOUNGE
00843144 .... $14.99

96. LATIN JAZZ STANDARDS
00843145 .... $14.99

97. MAYBE I'M AMAZED
00843148 .... $15.99

98. DAVE FRISHBERG
00843149 .... $15.99

99. SWINGING STANDARDS
00843150 .... $14.99

100. LOUIS ARMSTRONG
00740423 .... $15.99

101. BUD POWELL
00843152 .... $14.99

102. JAZZ POP
00843153 .... $14.99

103. ON GREEN DOLPHIN STREET & OTHER JAZZ CLASSICS
00843154 .... $14.99

104. ELTON JOHN
00843155 .... $14.99

105. SOULFUL JAZZ
00843151 .... $15.99

106. SLO' JAZZ
00843117 .... $14.99

107. MOTOWN CLASSICS
00843116 .... $14.99

108. JAZZ WALTZ
00843159 .... $15.99

109. OSCAR PETERSON
00843160 .... $15.99

110. JUST STANDARDS
00843161 .... $15.99

111. COOL CHRISTMAS
00843162 .... $15.99

114. MODERN JAZZ QUARTET FAVORITES
00843163 .... $15.99

115. THE SOUND OF MUSIC
00843164 .... $15.99

116. JACO PASTORIUS
00843165 .... $15.99

117. ANTONIO CARLOS JOBIM – MORE HITS
00843166 .... $15.99

118. BIG JAZZ STANDARDS COLLECTION
00843167 .... $27.50

119. JELLY ROLL MORTON
00843168 .... $15.99

120. J.S. BACH
00843169 .... $15.99

121. DJANGO REINHARDT
00843170 .... $15.99

122. PAUL SIMON
00843182 .... $16.99

123. BACHARACH & DAVID
00843185 .... $15.99

124. JAZZ-ROCK HORN HITS
00843186 .... $15.99

126. COUNT BASIE CLASSICS
00843157 .... $15.99

Prices, contents, and availability subject to change without notice.

FOR MORE INFORMATION, SEE YOUR LOCAL MUSIC DEALER, OR WRITE TO:

HAL•LEONARD® CORPORATION
7777 W. BLUEMOUND RD. P.O. BOX 13819
MILWAUKEE, WISCONSIN 53213

Visit Hal Leonard online at
www.halleonard.com
for complete songlists.

0910